Cryptocurrency

The Market Entry, Exit and Stop-Loss Trading Strategies that made me over $100,000

Chris Lambert

responsibility or blame be held against the publisher for any reparation, damages, or monetary loss due to the information herein, either directly or indirectly. Respective authors own all copyrights not held by the publisher. The information herein is offered for informational purposes solely, and is universal as so. The presentation of the information is without contract or any type of guarantee assurance.

The trademarks that are used are without any consent, and the publication of the trademark is without permission or backing by the trademark owner. All trademarks and brands within this book are for clarifying purposes only and are the owned by the owners themselves, not affiliated with this document.

Table of contents

Chapter 1 – Introduction 1

Chapter 2 - About the Series 4

Chapter 3 - Head and Shoulders 6

Chapter 4 – Double Bottom 13

Chapter 5 – Symmetrical Triangles 19

Chapter 6 – Ascending Triangle 25

Chapter 7 – Falling Wedge 30

Chapter 8 – Pole & Pennant 34

Chapter 9 – Flag 37

Chapter 10 – Bullish Rectangle 41

Conclusion 46

Chapter 1 – Introduction

This book focuses exclusively on the art of **Charting**, a technique of immense importance within the financial industry at large. Charting is based on the fundamental assumption stating that market prices follow predetermined and reoccurring patterns which can be spotted with the help of statistics, experience and market indices. Once recognized, these charts provide a good indication of a coin's short-term behavior.

Without a doubt, learning to recognize and dissect common chart patterns is the most reliable technique to profit from short-term trading, especially in the cryptocurrency markets. Many traders (including myself) have built entire careers around this art; I hope you will come to appreciate its powers very soon.

Unfortunately, the crypto markets contains a very large variety of chart patterns. As a trader, if you wish to make consistent and highly profitable trades you must become familiar with most of them – or at least the most common ones.

Throughout this book I will present the charting patterns most relevant to the beginner/intermediate-level trader. I will show you how to identify and recognize each pattern while trading, covering its unique features and behaviours.

Once you have recognized a pattern in the making, you must know exactly how to react (and quickly!). You are not gambling – every trade must be carefully planned in advance and executed without deviating from the plan. To help you in this aspect, I have carefully laid out my personal trading strategies in this book. For each pattern, I will show you…

- **Entry-Points (e.g. when to buy)**: Every chart has periods of uncertainty where it is hard to predict price fluctuations and other periods with a clear turning point (for instance, a breakout). I will show you the best positions to enter each pattern, avoiding uncertainty and leveraging turning points to your advantage – hence maximizing profits!
- **Stop-Loss Placement (e.g. cut your losses)**: Trading is never an exact science, and when things don't go as planned you must have a 'safety net' to protect yourself. The stop-loss is that safety net, it represents the *maximum amount you are willing to lose in a single trade*. For instance, "as soon as the price drops below 178.00$, I will sell all my positions and cut my losses". Ideas such as "I can make it all back" belong in Vegas! I will show you how to effectively place a stop-loss for every chart pattern, minimizing risk.

- **Exit Strategy** (e.g. **when to sell**): Developing an effective exit strategy can be extremely difficult, especially for new traders. You are in the middle of a clear, strong trend and your profits are increasing – why would you sell? This is called the **Fear of Missing Out** and causes traders to become sloppy, inaccurate and irrational – essentially gamblers. I use **measured objectives** to determine my exit price; when this is reached I take my profits home, no regrets. I will show you how to calculate measured objectives for all charts in a different number of scenarios.

After reading this book, many price fluctuations will no longer appear 'random'; you will begin to dissect every price variation systematically, looking for signs and indices that point to recognizable and predictable market behaviors (i.e. chart patterns). With experience, you can use this ability to build a highly profitable trading business. I, and many other traders, use these exact techniques every day to build fortunes.

Chapter 2 - About the Series

"Investing in Cryptocurrency" is the first instalment of the book series **Crypto Trading Secrets**, carefully developed by myself and my overachieving trainee James. The series was designed using a very pragmatic approach – **we only cover material that is directly relevant to trading cryptocurrency in today's markets.** All the tools, strategies and resources in this book were personally tested and implemented by myself at some stage of my career – I know they work, you will too!

Throughout the series I assume a high-school level knowledge in mathematics/statistics and only a rough exposure to economics and the cryptocurrency industry. Absolutely no previous experience in trading is required. Whenever we come across a new topic, concept or formula I will cover all the required material beforehand, maximizing and facilitating your learning process.

However, my explanations can only go *so far*. You need to understand this series will challenge your knowledge of the trading industry, covering many techniques you may have never thought possible.

Especially in later books, we will dive into more advanced trading techniques I have learned by working directly within the industry. To keep up with the material, I need you to be **committed** and **passionate** about the topics we will cover. It is absolutely necessary that you take action and actively implement the techniques presented in this book.

I have been working very hard on structuring the content of this series, but for now only the first publications have been officially released to the public – please visit my Author page for the latest releases (www.bit.ly/ChrisLambert). In the meantime, I would highly appreciate any feedback on the current publications and suggestions for future topics – please leave these in Amazon's official review section.

*Editor's Note: this is the second book of the series **Crypto Trading Secrets** – the author assumes a fundamental understanding of **Technical Analysis**. You should know what a support/resistance line is, what the Dow Theory dictates, how to read charts, how to identify and interpret market indices and familiarity with buyer/seller purchasing behaviors. These topics were covered in the first book of the series. The best online platforms for purchasing, trading and analyzing cryptocurrencies were also presented in the first publication.*

Chapter 3 - Head and Shoulders

This pattern appears frequently in the crypto markets and, if treated correctly, can lead to highly profitable trades. As the name suggests, the price chart will form the shape of two smaller peaks (shoulders) with a central larger peak (the head) – these are followed by a downwards breakout (i.e. sharp decrease in price). This pattern represents a **trend-reversal** – or the transition from a bullish market (increasing price) to bearish market (decreasing price).

Recognizing the Pattern

When the market is registering consecutive **higher peaks** in an upwards trend and are followed by a **lower high,** you may be in the middle of a head and shoulder pattern. For reference, a lower high occurs when a peak price is lower than the previous one, i.e. the **right shoulder.**

Most traders consider a head and shoulders pattern complete when the price falls below the **neckline**, as shown above. I find this approach inaccurate and unreliable – false breaks are extremely common (i.e. the price dips just below the neckline and rises back again).

Personally, I consider the pattern complete when there is also a **lower low**. In other words *"when the price falls below the previous minimum"*. At this point, I *expect* a downwards breakout to occur. On the following page, I show you exactly how I identify a head & shoulders pattern using real-market data.

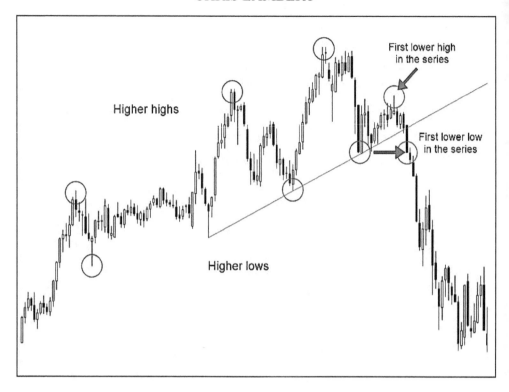

Higher highs

First lower high
in the series

First lower low
in the series

Higher lows

Entry-points

We have discussed the main features of the pattern and how it can be recognized, let's now discuss our entry strategy. Since we are expecting a decrease in price (downwards breakout), we will be **shorting** the market. Our aim is to sell our holdings before the breakout and buying them again after the price has dropped, for a profit.

When should we sell (or enter the market)? Personally, I place my sell orders just below the previous low. In other words, as soon as a new lower low occurs I sell all my holdings. This point is represented in the graph below.

Stop-Loss Placement

The stop-loss is a form of 'safety net' for traders. It is a boundary you place on the trade representing the **maximum amount you are willing to lose** if the market does not behave as you predicted – the *maximum risk associated with this trade*.

Personally, when trading the head and shoulders I place the stop-loss just above the right shoulder. Take a look below:

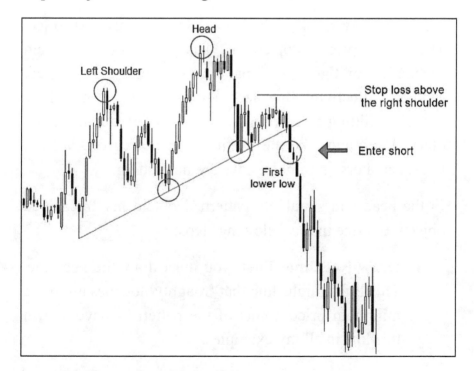

Exit Strategy

Developing effective exit strategies can be extremely difficult, especially for new traders. You are in the middle of a strong downtrend and your profits are increasing – why would you sell? In these circumstances the **Fear of Missing Out** is your biggest enemy; you become greedy and run the risk of losing all the profits of your trade.

At what point do you say 'now it's enough' and move on? You must have a well-crafted exit-strategy for every trade you make. Remember, profitable trades are all about planning and careful execution. This isn't Vegas – you are not a 'gambler' hoping to 'double up'!

I use **measured objectives** to determine my exit-price. These are price 'objectives' based on the size and fluctuation of the overall pattern. They are a structured, rigid and effective selling technique to avoid greed and the 'hope' of hitting more profits. When the price reaches my object I sell and take the profit home, no regrets. We are not speculators or gamblers, we are not betting.

In the head and shoulders pattern, I obtain my 'measured objective' price in the following steps:

1. **Draw Neckline:** First, you must draw the neckline. This is a straight-line that 'roughly' touches all of the minimum price points of the pattern. I have shown this line in all my examples.

2. **Vertical height of Head-Neckline:** You must then calculate the vertical height between the neckline and the head (maximum price reached).

3. **Subtract from Breakout point:** Now, you must wait until the price breaks the neckline. At this point, subtract the distance calculated in the previous step – this gives you the 'measured objective' price. Again, I recommend waiting for a lower low before entering the market.

The figure below shows all of the steps.

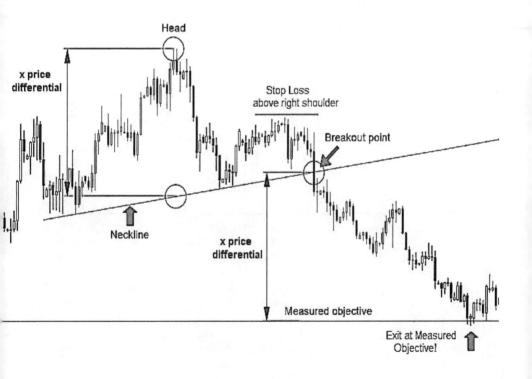

Inverse Head and shoulders

The inverse head and shoulders is a variation of the pattern discussed in this chapter – in fact it is the symmetrical opposite. You can approach it in the same way using the same trading strategies we just discussed. Here is an example of the inverse head and shoulder chart pattern:

Chapter 4 – Double Bottom

The Pattern

The Double Bottom is one of the most fundamental and well-recognized chart patterns. It is a trend-reversal pattern, signaling the change of a market from bearish (downwards trend) to bullish (upwards trend).

The pattern is characterized by a strong downtrend terminating in two equal lows, followed by an upwards breakout - the two lows form a very strong support line. The maximum price (high) reached between the two lows is another important feature – it defines the neckline and is used to determine entry and exit strategies.

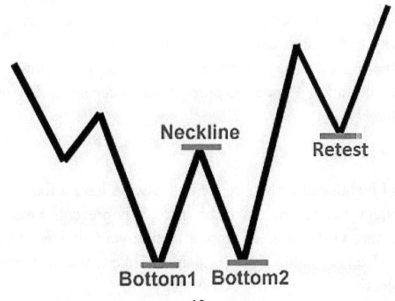

Neckline

Retest

Bottom1 Bottom2

Conservative Approach

First, we will discuss the 'conservative' trading approach for the double top chart pattern. I recommend new traders follow this approach as it is more reliable and requires less experience, or as we call it *'instinct'*.

Entry Points

Generally, the pattern is considered **confirmed** only the price breaches the neckline – we can expect a breakout to occur thereafter. In this approach we do not make a move before this signal has arrived, we are waiting 'formal confirmation' of the pattern. Hence, *we place a **buy order** just above the neckline.*

Stop-loss Placement

It can be difficult to effectively place a stop-loss in the double bottom pattern – usually you will find there are many fluctuations and retests during breakout. I like to be extra conservative and place my stop-loss just below the 'two bottoms'. Hence, *we place a **sell order** just below the support line.*

Exit Strategy

As I mentioned earlier, you should always have a fixed exit strategy before you make the trade; this prevents **Fear of Missing Out** and greed from affecting your choices. As in the Head & Shoulder pattern before, I like to use **measured objectives** to define my exit strategy:

1. **Draw Neckline:** First, you must draw identify the neckline. In the double bottom pattern this is relatively straightforward: it is a horizontal line located at the maximum price between the two bottoms.

2. **Vertical height of Bottoms-Neckline:** You must then calculate the vertical height between the neckline and the two bottoms.

3. **Add to Neckline**: Add this vertical height to the neckline to determine your exit price. Hence, *we place a **sell order** at the exit price.*

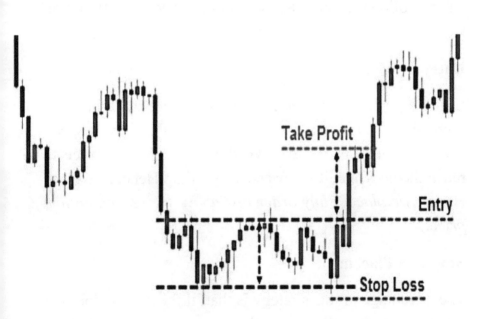

Aggressive Approach

In this approach we make a mover before the pattern is 'officially confirmed' – if correct, we obtain much greater profits. However, it is much more difficult to predict market behavior before we receive 'official confirmation' of the pattern. However, in this strategy we can afford to place a stop-loss very close to our entry-position – minimizing risk in case we are wrong.

Personally, I prefer this strategy to trade on the double bottom pattern, but I do not recommend it to those without experience. Recognizing chart patterns is a difficult enough when following all the guidelines and 'confirmation signals' – with only 'partial information' is even harder.

Entry Strategy

If it's a double bottom pattern, the price will increase immediately after the second bottom – this is where we want to make our move. We don't wait for the price to reach the neckline, it's a 'waste of profits'. Hence, we place Hence, *we place a **buy order** just above the second bottom price.*

Stop-loss Placement

The advantage of this strategy is that, if the pattern does not follow as expected you will now immediately. This is because you entered immediately after bottom 2. If the price increases above the neckline you were right; if the price drops any further you know you were wrong and the pattern will not follow through – you can sell immediately. Hence, you have an extremely small trade risk associated with this trade. *We place a **buy order** just above the second bottom price.*

Exit Strategy

We calculate our measured objective as in the previous strategy:

1. **Draw Neckline**
2. **Measure Vertical height of Bottoms-Neckline**
3. **Add to Neckline & place sell order**

The Double Top Chart

This pattern is a variation of the double bottom chart we just discussed. All of the features and chart analysis techniques remain the same, but are simply inverted. Here is an example below:

Chapter 5 – Symmetrical Triangles

The pattern

Triangles are an extremely common and popular way to organize trades. There are a number of triangle-based chart patterns, but in this chapter we will focus exclusively on the symmetrical triangle pattern.

The price is bound by two slanted support and resistance lines, taking up the shape of a symmetrical triangle pattern. Once the price reaches the apex of the triangle, a breakout typically occurs, but its direction is typically unknown. In fact, this pattern signals *stabilization* and *uncertainty* in the market: there is no clear trend or direction in the price. On the following page you will find a typical example of a symmetrical triangle pattern.

Conservative Approach - Wait for Retest

This pattern is caused by uncertainty and price stabilization – how can 'uncertainty' help us make money? The answer is: *we wait for a breakout and then make a move.*

However, there is one thing we must beware of: the **false breakout.** This is a common feature of the pattern: the price breaks out of the triangle slightly, but pulls back into it afterwards (without any real breakout). If we make a move before a false breakout, we stand a good chance of losing profits.

Waiting for a **retest** reduces the chances of investing in a false breakout. In fact, most symmetrical triangle breakouts occur in a similar pattern: price breaches triangle boundary (i.e. breakout price), there is a moderate price increase, the price pulls back to the breakout point followed by a much larger price increase. This final price increase is what gives you the most profits and where we want to invest in!

Entry Points

First we must wait for the price to breach the triangle boundary and the following price increase. The retest occurs when the price pulls back to the original breakout price. Hence, *we place a **buy order** just above breakout price*

Stop-Loss

The main advantage of this strategy is that we can operate on a very small stop-loss, giving us a very small risk of trade. We know that if the price pulls back into the triangle boundaries, it was a false breakout. Hence, *we place a **sell order** at the triangle boundary below the retest point.*

Exit Strategy

As with all previous trades, we will use *measured objectives* to locate our exit-point. For symmetrical triangles the procedure is the following:

1. **Measure Vertical height of triangle opening**: You must go to the opening of the triangle and measure its vertical height.
2. **Extend this distance from breakout point**: add this vertical height to the breakout point, *we place a sell order at this price.*

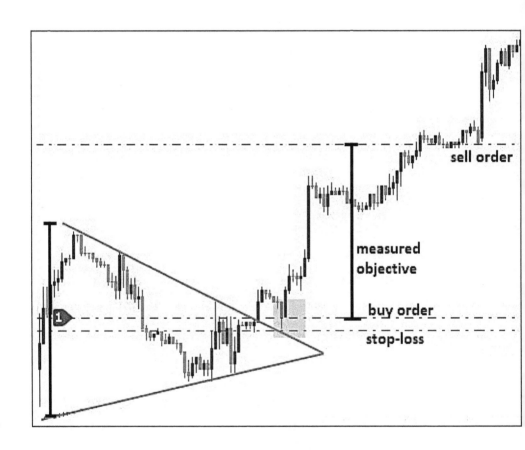

Aggressive Approach

This is my preferred option to trade the symmetrical triangle pattern. You are taking the full risks of a false breakout, but can expect much greater profits. Also, it can be quite difficult to perfectly track and monitor retests.

From my past trading on different markets (e.g. forex/penny stocks), I used to follow the conservative approach when dealing with symmetrical triangles. However, the cryptocurrency markets are highly volatile in nature and I find false breakouts much more infrequently.

Entry Points

We make a move as soon as the price breaks outside the triangle. If the price breaks above, we expect a sharp increase in price; if the price breaks below, we expect a sharp decrease in price. Unfortunately you cannot place automatic orders for this, you will have to monitor and make decisions live (more time-intensive)

Stop-Loss

Given our fast entry-strategy, we may face significant price fluctuations as the market stabilizes and further progresses. Therefore, our stop-loss must be wide enough to accommodate for these fluctuations. In this scenario, you must locate where the breakout occurred and place the stop-loss on the opposite edge of the triangle. Hence, *we place a sell order at the opposing edge of the triangle.*

Exit Strategy

We calculate our measured objective, hence exit strategy, exactly as in conservative approach:

3. **Measure Vertical height of triangle opening**
4. **Extend this distance from breakout point**: *we place a sell order at this price.*

Chapter 6 – Ascending Triangle

The Pattern

The ascending triangle is a variation of the symmetrical triangle chart described in the previous chapter. In this version the top edge is flat, forming a flat resistance line. It shows a strong and growing buyer interest against a decreasing and weakening buyer interest. Approaching the end (or apex) of the triangle you will usually find a sharp upwards breakout.

I see these charts very often in the crypto markets, however new and inexperienced traders may have difficult identifying them. In fact, ascending triangles are often very faint and broad – you will rarely find an 'obvious' ascending triangle. My recommendation is to make very light trades on these charts at first and gradually increase with experience. You can find an example of a typical ascending triangle on the following page.

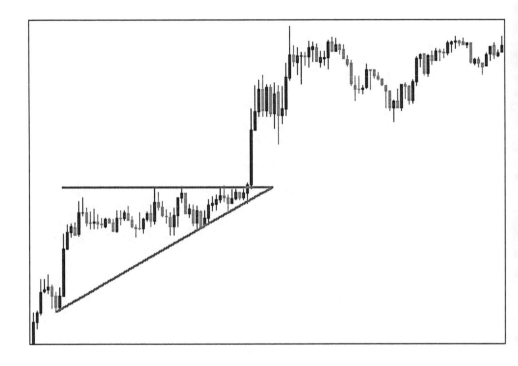

Entry Points

When recognized correctly, ascending triangles are a very reliable and accurate chart pattern. I like to enter the trade as soon as the price breaks the resistance line. Hence, *we place a buy order just above the resistance line.*

There is the possibility of a false breakout occurring, but in the crypto markets I find this occurs only rarely for ascending patterns and can be ignored. If you wish to trade ascending patterns using a retest you can, but personally I think this is unnecessary and will make your trades less frequent and less profitable

Stop-Loss

In the ascending triangle pattern, you must find the opposite edge of the triangle, at the point where breakout occurred. Hence, *we place a **sell order** at this price.*

Exit Strategy

As you well know, we must now calculate the **measured objective** – this will give us the measured objective. The procedure is the same as already described for the symmetrical triangle:

1. **Measure Vertical height of triangle opening**: You must go to the opening of the triangle and measure its vertical height.
2. **Add distance to support line**: add this height to the breakout point, *we place a sell order at this price.*

You can find all of the above strategies and steps represented on the graph below.

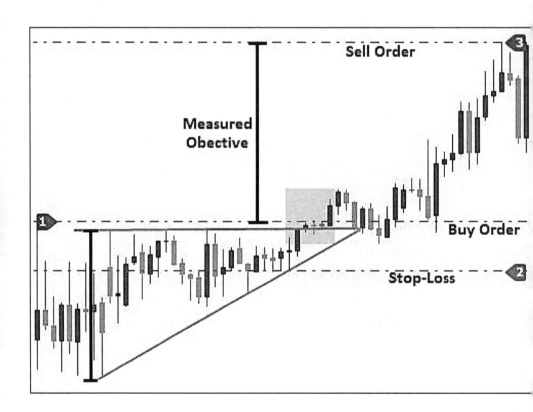

Descending Triangle

The descending triangle is another commonly used triangle pattern. It signals a loss of power from the buyers and increasing power from the sellers. It is built on a flat support line and a slanted resistance – upon completion of the pattern we can expect a sharp downwards breakout. Take a look at this variation below:

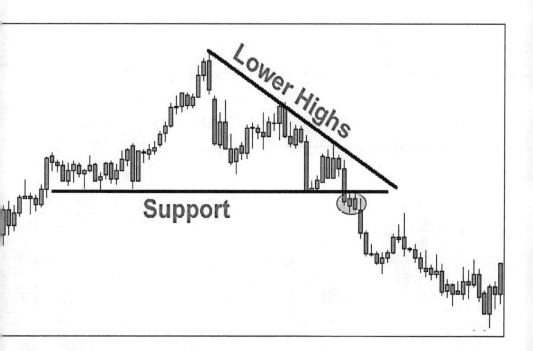

Chapter 7 – Falling Wedge

The Pattern

At first sight, the falling wedge pattern appears similar to random, downward price fluctuations.　Upon further consideration, you will notice that the fluctuations are bound by two decreasing trend-lines, with the top line having a steeper gradient – this creates the image of a 'falling wedge'.

The downwards trend leads up to an upwards breakout, where a sharp price increase is observed. As traders, we use this to make a significant profit. Here is an example of a typical falling wedge pattern:

Entry Points

I recommend entering the falling wedge pattern once the top boundary line is breached. I recommend you personally assess the trade and do not use a buy order. Hence, *we make the **buy order** at breakout point.*

As already discussed in previous chapters, **false breakouts** are a significant risk. However, even I have only seen these rarely when trading the falling wedge pattern on crypto markets. On Forex they are much more common, but we are dealing with a very different beast. If you are worried about a potential breakout, I suggest waiting for a retest to make your buy order (I have discussed a similar technique in the chapter covering symmetrical triangles).

Stop-Loss

Stop-loss placement is an extremely important part of all trades, especially since we are not waiting for a retest and hence must leave a greater margin for fluctuation. My approach is to find the breakout point and place the stop-loss on the opposite edge. Hence, *we place a **sell order** on the support line at the breakout point.*

Exit Strategy

Now we can move on to the best part: taking away the profits! The way I calculate the measured objective for this pattern is the following:

1. **Measure the vertical height of the wedge opening**: find the vertical opening of the wedge and measure this height (i.e. the maximum difference in price between the support and resistance lines.
2. **Add this height to the breakout point**: add this vertical distance to the breakout price. Hence, *place a sell order at this price.*

Rising Wedge

The rising wedge represents a variation of the falling wedge. The fluctuations in price exhibit an overall positive trend, but are ultimately followed by a negative breakout (sharp decrease in price). Take a look below:

Chapter 8 – Pole & Pennant

The Pattern

The pole & pennant is a chart pattern characterized by a very sharp increase in price (known as the 'pole') followed by a momentary pause in the market (known as the 'pennant'). Upon completion of the pattern, the strong uptrend typically resumes. The price increase that follows is typically equal to the size of the 'pole'. This pattern is particularly important because it allows you to enter the market in the middle of strong uptrend.

The size of the pennant can be very small in comparison to the 'pole', which makes this pattern difficult to recognize. In particular, in the middle of a strong uptrend new traders may be overtake by greed and the Fear of Missing Out – you must remain calm and assess all patterns objectively.

Entry Points

I recommend entering the market as soon as the price breaches the boundaries of the pennant. Hence, *we make our buy order*.

Of course, the pennant signifies a time of stabilization and uncertainty for the market – you should allow 'reasonable' time for the market to stabilize before making a purchase. I used 'reasonable', because this period varies on the historical data you are using. For instance, if the pattern spans a timeframe of 1-week, I would wait 6-12 hours before making a move.

Stop-Loss

We must now decide where to place the stop-loss. Since the pennant represents a time of stabilization and is relatively small in scale, I prefer a lenient and accommodating stop-loss. I tend to place the stop-loss roughly halfway along the pennant's support line. Hence, *we place a sell order at this price*.

Exit Strategy

We calculate the sell price of this pattern in a slightly different way: our measured objective is given by the total height of the pole. Afterwards we add add this height to the breakout price of the pennant, hence *we place a sell order at this price.*

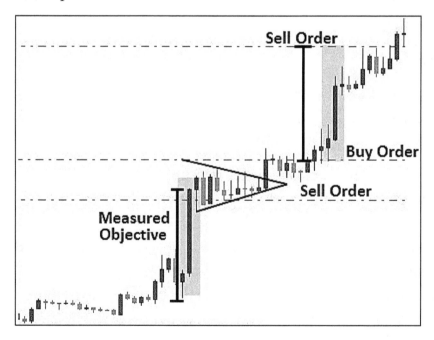

Chapter 9 – Flag

The Pattern

The flag pattern is fundamentally very similar to the pennant we discussed in the previous chapter. The flag also represents a momentary period of market stabilization in response to strong and sudden price increase. Upon completion of the pattern, we can expect a continuation of the original strong price uptrend. During this time of stabilization the price fluctuates between two mildly decreasing resistance and support lines, resembling the shape of a flag.

It is important you learn to recognize this pattern, because it gives you the opportunity to enter in the middle of strong price uptrend. A typical example of a flag pattern is shown on the next page.

Entry Points

You should enter the trade once the price breaches beyond the flag boundaries. At this price, *we make a buy order.*

As I have already mentioned, you must be aware of the potential risks of a **false breakout**. Again, I do not see false breakouts often in this type of pattern, but if you are new to trading you should take some precautions to protect yourself. As before, I simply recommend waiting a 'reasonable' amount of time after the breakout. Alternatively you can wait for a retest to make your purchase, but this highly conservative approach may cause you to miss out on many potentially profitable trades.

Stop-Loss

The flag is a fundamentally narrow and, before the breakout, a fairly unstable pattern – it is important you allow enough room for price stabilization. Some traders I know place it midway through the support line, although I have personally missed out on profitable trades using this approach. Hence, I now place the stop-loss below the flag support line.

Exit Strategy

We must now calculate the **measured objective** for the pattern. I cannot stress the importance of having a predefined sell price in mind. You are not gambling, you are trading – every choice you make should be calculated and programmed in advance. You should not leave anything to chance. The measured objective is equal to the total price increase before the final flag pattern commenced. Add this to the breakout point; *at this price we place a sell order*.

All of the above steps and strategies are represented on the graph below.

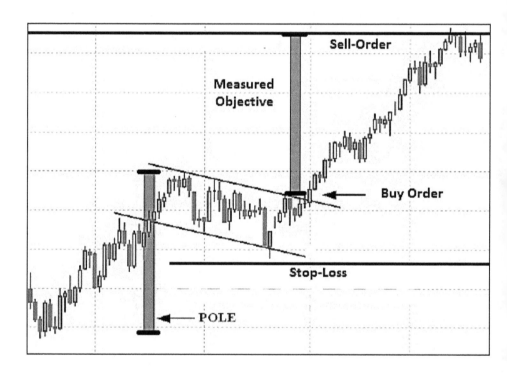

Chapter 10 – Bullish Rectangle

The Pattern

The eighth and final pattern we will discuss in this book is the bullish rectangle pattern. This is yet another bullish continuation pattern and is fundamentally very similar to previous two patterns we just discussed: the flag and the pole & pennant.

As I already explained, when there is a very sharp price increase in the market there is usually a momentary period of uncertainty & stabilization that takes place. In the rectangular pattern, we see the price bouncing between two flat boundaries: a support line and a resistance line. As the price breaks through the resistance line an upwards breakout occurs, bringing a significant increase in market price. Amongst all the bullish continuation patterns discussed, this is perhaps the easiest to recognize.

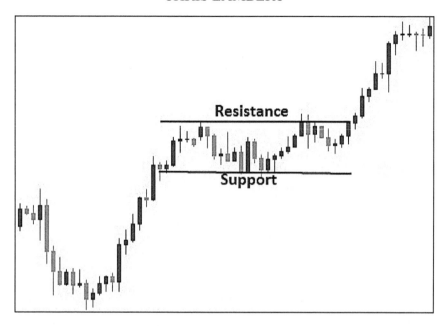

Entry Points

Once the price breaks the resistance line *we can place a buy order.*

However, for this pattern in particular I recommend waiting until the breakout becomes 'obvious'. I have seen many 'false breakouts' appearing in this pattern and therefore I suggest you approach this with significant awareness.

Stop-Loss

When trading on a rectangle pattern I like to allow enough room for price fluctuations. Therefore, *I place the stop-loss below the support line.* If you are feeling more conservative or unsure about your decision, you can place the stop-loss slightly above the support line.

Exit Strategy

We must now determine our target objective for the trade, deciding a price at which to sell our holdings. To do this, measure the height of the rectangle (i.e. the difference in price between the support and resistance). Add this distance to the resistance line, *at this price we place a sell order.*

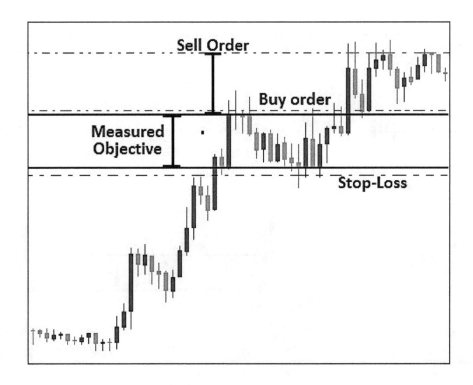

Bearish Rectangle

The Bearish rectangle is a simple variation of the bullish Rectangle discussed in this chapter. In fact, the features and appearance of the chart remain largely unchanged – only the placement of the pattern changes. This version of the rectangle is in fact a bearish continuation pattern, i.e. it is preceded by a strong decreasing price trend and followed by further price decrease. Take a look below:

TRADING CRYPTOCURRENCY

Conclusion

Dear Reader,

I have devoted a lot of time and effort towards writing this book – I would like to thank you for reaching this point.

By trading in cryptocurrency I have built a small fortune from nothing and my life has changed forever. My most recent goal is to share this knowledge and my experiences with anyone willing to listen, in the hope of motivating and leading as many people as possible towards financial success like myself.

I hope that, having completed this book, you feel more confident and conscious of trading in cryptocurrencies and are now ready to take on this challenge head on!

I know that I have repeated this multiple times throughout the book, but it is an extremely important truth and you must understand its full implications: **trading is a skill and like all skills it takes time to develop**.

If your first trades are not successful do not despair. Keep practicing, improving yourself, studying and learning from your mistakes – crypto trading is real career and if you have the enough determination and drive you can become rich dong it!

In conclusion, I hope you have found my work useful and that it will soon bring you extensive financial success.

Yours Truly,

Chris Lambert

CPSIA information can be obtained
at www.ICGtesting.com
Printed in the USA
LVHW03s2219110618
580407LV00001B/97/P

9 781978 302815